Connected  Mathematics™

Growing, Growing, Growing

Exponential Relationships

Student Edition

Glenda Lappan
James T. Fey
William M. Fitzgerald
Susan N. Friel
Elizabeth Difanis Phillips

Prentice
Hall

Glenview, Illinois
Needham, Massachusetts
Upper Saddle River, New Jersey

Connected Mathematics™ was developed at Michigan State University with the support of National Science Foundation Grant No. MDR 9150217.

This project was supported, in part,
by the
National Science Foundation
Opinions expressed are those of the authors
and not necessarily those of the Foundation

The Michigan State University authors and administration have agreed that all MSU royalties arising from this publication will be devoted to purposes supported by the Department of Mathematics and the MSU Mathematics Education Enrichment Fund.

Photo Acknowledgements: 11 © Laima Druskis/Stock, Boston; 22 © Bill Bachmann/Photo Researchers, Inc.; 31 © Schuster/Superstock, Inc.; 38 (wolf) © D. Northcott/Superstock, Inc.; 38 (fly) Dr. Jeremy Burgess/SPL/Photo Researchers, Inc.; 43 © Charles Gupton/Tony Stone Images; 45 © Robert E. Daemmrich/Tony Stone Images; 48 © Lynn Lennon/Photo Researchers, Inc.

ISBN 0-13-053079-4

1 2 3 4 5 6 7 8 9 10   05 04 03 02 01

The Connected Mathematics Project Staff

Project Directors

James T. Fey
University of Maryland

William M. Fitzgerald
Michigan State University

Susan N. Friel
University of North Carolina at Chapel Hill

Glenda Lappan
Michigan State University

Elizabeth Difanis Phillips
Michigan State University

Project Manager

Kathy Burgis
Michigan State University

Technical Coordinator

Judith Martus Miller
Michigan State University

Curriculum Development Consultants

David Ben-Chaim
Weizmann Institute

Alex Friedlander
Weizmann Institute

Eleanor Geiger
University of Maryland

Jane Miller
University of Maryland

Jane Mitchell
University of North Carolina at Chapel Hill

Anthony D. Rickard
Alma College

Collaborating Teachers/Writers

Mary K. Bouck
Portland, Michigan

Jacqueline Stewart
Okemos, Michigan

Graduate Assistants

Scott J. Baldridge
Michigan State University

Angie S. Eshelman
Michigan State University

M. Faaiz Gierdien
Michigan State University

Jane M. Keiser
Indiana University

Angela S. Krebs
Michigan State University

James M. Larson
Michigan State University

Ronald Preston
Indiana University

Tat Ming Sze
Michigan State University

Sarah Theule-Lubienski
Michigan State University

Jeffrey J. Wanko
Michigan State University

Evaluation Team

Mark Hoover
Michigan State University

Diane V. Lambdin
Indiana University

Sandra K. Wilcox
Michigan State University

Judith S. Zawojewski
National-Louis University

Teacher/Assessment Team

Kathy Booth
Waverly, Michigan

Anita Clark
Marshall, Michigan

Julie Faulkner
Traverse City, Michigan

Theodore Gardella
Bloomfield Hills, Michigan

Yvonne Grant
Portland, Michigan

Linda R. Lobue
Vista, California

Suzanne McGrath
Chula Vista, California

Nancy McIntyre
Troy, Michigan

Mary Beth Schmitt
Traverse City, Michigan

Linda Walker
Tallahassee, Florida

Software Developer

Richard Burgis
East Lansing, Michigan

Development Center Directors

Nicholas Branca
San Diego State University

Dianne Briars
Pittsburgh Public Schools

Frances R. Curcio
New York University

Perry Lanier
Michigan State University

J. Michael Shaughnessy
Portland State University

Charles Vonder Embse
Central Michigan University

Special thanks to the students and teachers at these pilot schools!

Baker Demonstration School
Evanston, Illinois

Bertha Vos Elementary School
Traverse City, Michigan

Blair Elementary School
Traverse City, Michigan

Bloomfield Hills Middle School
Bloomfield Hills, Michigan

Brownell Elementary School
Flint, Michigan

Catlin Gabel School
Portland, Oregon

Cherry Knoll Elementary School
Traverse City, Michigan

Cobb Middle School
Tallahassee, Florida

Courtade Elementary School
Traverse City, Michigan

Duke School for Children
Durham, North Carolina

DeVeaux Junior High School
Toledo, Ohio

East Junior High School
Traverse City, Michigan

Eastern Elementary School
Traverse City, Michigan

Eastlake Elementary School
Chula Vista, California

Eastwood Elementary School
Sturgis, Michigan

Elizabeth City Middle School
Elizabeth City, North Carolina

Franklinton Elementary School
Franklinton, North Carolina

Frick International Studies Academy
Pittsburgh, Pennsylvania

Gundry Elementary School
Flint, Michigan

Hawkins Elementary School
Toledo, Ohio

Hilltop Middle School
Chula Vista, California

Holmes Middle School
Flint, Michigan

Interlochen Elementary School
Traverse City, Michigan

Los Altos Elementary School
San Diego, California

Louis Armstrong Middle School
East Elmhurst, New York

McTigue Junior High School
Toledo, Ohio

National City Middle School
National City, California

Norris Elementary School
Traverse City, Michigan

Northeast Middle School
Minneapolis, Minnesota

Oak Park Elementary School
Traverse City, Michigan

Old Mission Elementary School
Traverse City, Michigan

Old Orchard Elementary School
Toledo, Ohio

Portland Middle School
Portland, Michigan

Reizenstein Middle School
Pittsburgh, Pennsylvania

Sabin Elementary School
Traverse City, Michigan

Shepherd Middle School
Shepherd, Michigan

Sturgis Middle School
Sturgis, Michigan

Terrell Lane Middle School
Louisburg, North Carolina

Tierra del Sol Middle School
Lakeside, California

Traverse Heights Elementary School
Traverse City, Michigan

University Preparatory Academy
Seattle, Washington

Washington Middle School
Vista, California

Waverly East Intermediate School
Lansing, Michigan

Waverly Middle School
Lansing, Michigan

West Junior High School
Traverse City, Michigan

Willow Hill Elementary School
Traverse City, Michigan

Contents

Growing, Growing, Growing

A veterinarian can give a pet medicine to relieve the discomfort of flea bites. The effects of such medicines wear off in a predictable pattern. Suppose that each day after an injection, the amount of medicine in a dog's blood is $\frac{3}{4}$ the amount of the previous day. After how many days will less than half of the original dose remain in the dog's blood?

JOE OWEN Tri-

COUGARS

Nicole is studying the growth of a beetle population. She begins her experiment with five beetles and finds that the population doubles each month. What would a graph of the number of beetles over a year's time look like?

When Ella was in sixth grade, she invested $500 in a low-risk stock. Ella has just graduated from high school and wants to sell her stock to help pay for a trip to Italy. If the value of the stock has increased by 5% each year since Ella bought it, how much is her stock now worth?

One of the most important uses of algebra is to model patterns of change. You are already familiar with linear patterns of change. Linear patterns are characterized by constant differences and straight-line graphs. In a table for a linear relationship, a constant amount is added to the y value each time the x value increases by 1.

In this unit, you will study exponential patterns of change. In a table for an exponential relationship, the y value is multiplied by a constant amount each time the x value increases by 1. Exponential patterns are fascinating because, although the values may change gradually at first, they eventually increase or decrease very rapidly.

Mathematical Highlights

In *Growing, Growing, Growing* you will explore one of the most important types of non-linear relations among variables—exponential functions. The unit should help you to

● Recognize situations where one variable is an exponential function of another variable;

● Recognize the connections between exponential equations and patterns in tables and graphs of those relations;

● Construct equations to express exponential patterns that appear in data tables, graphs, and problem conditions;

● Use tables, graphs, and equations of exponential relations to solve problems about exponential growth and decay in a variety of situations from science and business; and

● Compare exponential and linear relationships.

As you work on the problems of this unit, make it a habit to ask questions about problem situations that involve non-linear relations: *Is the relationship among variables in this situation an example of exponential growth or decay? What equation would model the data or the pattern in a graph relating the variables? How could I answer the questions of the situation by studying a table or graph of the exponential relation?*

Exponential Growth

Repeated doubling, tripling, and quadrupling are types of exponential growth. In this investigation, you are introduced to exponential growth as you cut paper in half over and over and meet a very smart peasant from the ancient kingdom of Montarck. You will compare exponential growth with linear growth and explore exponential patterns in tables, graphs, and equations.

1.1 Making Ballots

Alejandro is making ballots for an election. He starts by cutting a sheet of paper in half. He then stacks the two pieces and cuts them in half. He stacks the resulting four pieces and cuts them in half. He repeats this process, creating smaller and smaller pieces of paper.

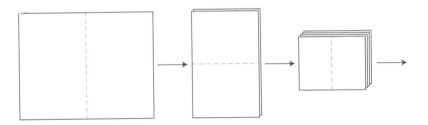

After each cut, Alejandro counts the ballots and records the results in a table.

Cuts	Ballots
1	2
2	4
3	
4	
5	

Alejandro wants to find a way to predict the number of ballots after any number of cuts.

Problem 1.1

A. Cut a sheet of paper as Alejandro did, and count the ballots after each cut. Make a table to show the number of ballots after 1 cut, 2 cuts, 3 cuts, and so on.

B. Look for a pattern in the way the number of ballots changes with each cut. Use your observations to extend your table to show the number of ballots for up to 10 cuts.

C. If Alejandro made 20 cuts, how many ballots would he have? How many ballots would he have if he made 30 cuts?

D. A stack of 250 sheets of the paper Alejandro is using is 1 inch high. How high would a stack of ballots be after 20 cuts? After 30 cuts?

E. How many cuts would Alejandro need to make to have a stack of ballots 1 foot high?

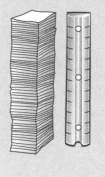

■ Problem 1.1 Follow-Up

When you found the number of ballots made by 10, 20, and 30 cuts, you probably found yourself multiplying long strings of 2s. Instead of writing out long product strings of the same factor, you can use **exponential form**. For example, you can write $2 \times 2 \times 2 \times 2 \times 2$ as 2^5, which is read "2 to the fifth power." In the expression 2^5, 2 is the **base** and 5 is the **exponent**. When you evaluate 2^5, you get $2^5 = 2 \times 2 \times 2 \times 2 \times 2 = 32$. We say that 32 is the **standard form** for 2^5.

1. Write each expression in exponential form.
   a. $2 \times 2 \times 2$
   b. $5 \times 5 \times 5 \times 5$
   c. $1.5 \times 1.5 \times 1.5 \times 1.5 \times 1.5 \times 1.5 \times 1.5$

2. Write each expression in standard form.
   a. 2^7 **b.** 3^3 **c.** 4.2^3

3. Most calculators have a $\boxed{\wedge}$ or $\boxed{y^x}$ key for evaluating exponents. Find out how to use your calculator to evaluate exponents, and then write each of these expressions in standard form.
   a. 2^{15} **b.** 3^{10} **c.** 1.5^{20}

4. Explain how the expressions 5^2, 2^5, and 5×2 differ.

5. You know that $5^2 = 25$. How can you use this fact to evaluate 5^4?

6. The standard form for 5^{10} is 9,765,625. How can you use this fact to evaluate 5^{11}?

1.2 Requesting a Reward

One day in the ancient kingdom of Montarek, a peasant saved the life of the king's daughter. The king was so grateful that he told the peasant she could have any reward she desired. The peasant—who was also the kingdom's chess champion—made an unusual request:

"I would like you to place 1 ruba on the first square of a chessboard, 2 rubas on the second square, 4 on the third square, 8 on the fourth square, and so on, until you have covered all 64 squares. Each square should have twice as many rubas as the previous square."

The king replied, "Rubas are the least valuable coin in the kingdom. Surely you can think of a better reward." But the peasant insisted, so the king agreed to her request.

Problem 1.2

A. Make a table showing the number of rubas the king will place on squares 1 through 16 of the chessboard.

B. How does the number of rubas change from one square to the next?

C. How many rubas will be on square 20? On square 30? On square 64?

D. What is the first square on which the king will place at least 1 million rubas?

E. If a Montarek ruba had the value of a U.S. penny, what would be the dollar values of the rubas on squares 10, 20, 30, 40, 50, and 60?

■ Problem 1.2 Follow-Up

1. Graph the (number of the square, number of rubas) data for squares 1 to 10. As the number of the square increases, how does the number of rubas change? What does this pattern of change tell you about the peasant's reward?

2. Write an equation for the relationship between the number of the square, n, and the number of rubas, r.

3. If a chessboard had 100 squares, how many rubas would be on square 100?

4. The pattern of change in the number of ballots in Problem 1.1 and the pattern of change in the number of rubas in this problem show **exponential growth.**

    a. How are the patterns of change in these two situations similar?

    b. Write an equation for the relationship between the number of ballots, b, and the number of cuts, n, in Problem 1.1.

1.3 Making a New Offer

When the king told the queen about the reward he had promised the peasant, the queen said, "You have promised her more money than we have in the entire royal treasury! You must convince her to accept a different reward."

After much contemplation, the king thought of a plan. He would create a new board with only 16 squares. He would place 1 ruba on the first square, 3 on the next, 9 on the next, and so on. Each square would have three times as many rubas as the previous square.

Problem 1.3

A. In the table below, plan 1 is the reward requested by the peasant, and plan 2 is the king's new plan. Copy and complete the table to show the number of rubas on squares 1 to 16 for each plan.

Square	Number of rubas	
	Plan 1	Plan 2
1	1	1
2	2	3
3	4	9
4		

B. How is the pattern of change in the number of rubas under plan 2 similar to and different from the pattern of change in the number of rubas under plan 1?

C. Write an equation for the relationship between the number of the square, n, and the number of rubas, r, for plan 2.

D. Is the total reward under the king's plan greater than or less than the total reward under the peasant's plan? How did you decide?

Problem 1.3 Follow-Up

1. Make a graph of plan 2 for $n = 1$ to 10. How does your graph compare to the graph you made for plan 1?

The queen devised a third reward that the king could offer the peasant. Under plan 3, the king would make a board with 12 squares. He would start with 1 ruba in the first square and quadruple the number of rubas from one square to the next. So, the pattern of rubas would be 1, 4, 16, 64, and so on.

2. Make a graph of plan 3 for $n = 1$ to 10. How does this graph compare to the graphs of plans 1 and 2?

3. Write an equation for the relationship between the number of the square, n, and the number of rubas, r, for plan 3. How do the equations for the three plans compare?

4. Of the three plans, which is best for the peasant? Which is best for the king?

5. Design another reward plan with a pattern of change that you think shows exponential growth. Explain why you think the growth is exponential.

As you work on these ACE questions, use your calculator whenever you need it.

Applications

1. Cut a sheet of paper into thirds. Stack the three pieces, and cut the stack into thirds. Stack all the pieces, and cut that stack into thirds.

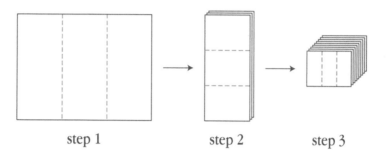

step 1   step 2   step 3

How many pieces of paper would you have at the end of

a. step 1   **b.** step 2   **c.** step 3

d. step 10   **e.** step n

2. While studying her family's history, Angie discovered records of ancestors 12 generations back. She wondered how many ancestors she had had in the past 12 generations. She decided to make a tree diagram to help her figure this out, but the diagram soon became very complex. Her diagram is shown on the next page.

   a. Make a table and a graph showing the number of ancestors Angie would find in each of the 12 generations.

   b. Write an equation for the number of ancestors, A, in a given generation, n.

   c. What is the total number of ancestors in all 12 generations?

   d. What similarities do you notice in the patterns of change for the number of ancestors, the number of ballots (Problem 1.1), and the number of rubas (Problems 1.2 and 1.3)? What differences do you notice?

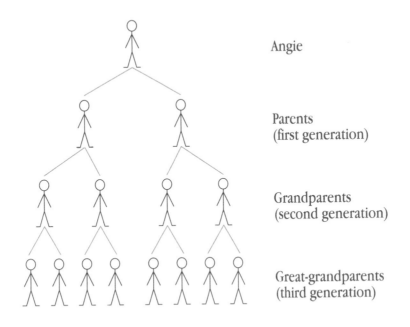

Angie

Parents
(first generation)

Grandparents
(second generation)

Great-grandparents
(third generation)

3. Many single-celled organisms reproduce by dividing into two identical cells. Suppose an amoeba divides into two amoebas every half hour.

a. A biologist starts an experiment with one amoeba. Make a table showing the number of amoebas she would have at the end of each hour over an 8-hour period.

b. Write an equation for the number of amoebas, *a*, after *t* hours.

c. How many hours will it take for the number of amoebas to reach 1 million?

d. Make a graph of the (time, amoebas) data from part a.

e. What similarities do you notice in the patterns of change for the number of amoebas and the number of ancestors (ACE question 2)? What differences do you notice?

In 4–6, write the expression in exponential form.

4. $2 \times 2 \times 2 \times 2$

5. $10 \times 10 \times 10 \times 10 \times 10 \times 10 \times 10$

6. $2.5 \times 2.5 \times 2.5 \times 2.5 \times 2.5$

In 7–9, write the expression in standard form.

7. 2^{10} **8.** 10^2 **9.** 3^9

Connections

10. A ruba had the same thickness as a modern U.S. penny (about 0.06 inch). Suppose the king had been able to reward the peasant by using plan 1 (doubling the number of rubas on each square).

    a. What would the height of the stack of rubas on square 64 have been?

    b. The average distance from Earth to the moon is about 240,000 miles. Which (if any) of the stacks of rubas would have reached the moon?

11. Consider these two equations, which involve exponential expressions:

    i. $R = 3^{n-1}$ **ii.** $R = 3^n - 1$

    a. For each equation, find R when n is 2.

    b. For each equation, find R when n is 10.

    c. Explain why the equations give different values of R for the same value of n.

12. Cesar said that since he can group $2 \times 2 \times 2 \times 2 \times 2 \times 2 \times 2 \times 2 \times 2 \times 2$ as $(2 \times 2 \times 2 \times 2) \times (2 \times 2 \times 2 \times 2 \times 2 \times 2)$, it must be true that $2^{10} = 2^4 \times 2^6$.

   a. Verify that Cesar is correct by evaluating both sides of the equation $2^{10} = 2^4 \times 2^6$.

   b. Use Cesar's idea of grouping factors to write three other expressions that are equivalent to 2^{10}. Evaluate each expression you find to verify that it is equivalent to 2^{10}.

   c. The standard form for 2^7 is 128, and the standard form for 2^5 is 32. Use these facts to evaluate 2^{12}. Show your work.

   d. Test Cesar's idea to see if it works for exponential expressions with other bases, such as 3^8 or 1.5^{11}. Test several cases. Give an argument supporting your conclusion.

   e. Find a general way to express Cesar's idea in words and with symbols.

Extensions

13. Molly figured out that $2^6 = 64$ and $4^3 = 64$. Then, since $2^2 = 4$, she substituted 2^2 for 4 in the expression 4^3 and got $(2^2)^3 = 64$. She said that since $2^6 = 64$ and $(2^2)^3 = 64$, it must be true that $(2^2)^3 = 2^6$.

   a. Verify that Molly is correct by evaluating both sides of the equation $(2^2)^3 = 2^6$.

   b. Use Molly's idea to find an exponential expression equivalent to the given expression.

      i. $(3^2)^4$ **ii.** $(4^3)^2$

   c. Find a general way to express Molly's idea in words and with symbols. Check your idea by testing it on three more examples.

14. Juan wrote out the first 12 powers of 2. He wrote $2^1 = 2$, $2^2 = 4$, $2^3 = 8$, and so on. He noticed a pattern in the digits in the units places of the results. He said he could use this pattern to predict the digit in the units place of 2^{100}.

    a. What pattern did Juan observe?

    b. What digit is in the units place of 2^{100}? Explain how you found your answer.

15. Here is a table like the one you made in Problem 1.1 with a row for 0 cuts added.

Cuts	Ballots
0	1
1	2
2	4
3	8
4	16

    a. Write an equation for the pattern in the table.

    b. Use your equation and the table to determine the value of 2^0.

    c. What do you think b^0 should equal for any number b, such as 3^0, 6^0, and 23^0? Check your idea with a calculator.

16. When the king of Montarek tried to figure out the total number of rubas he would have to reward the peasant under plan 1, he made a table like the one on the next page.

Square	Number of rubas on square	Total number of rubas
1	1	1
2	2	3
3	4	7
4		

a. Copy and complete the table for $n = 1$ to 10.

b. The king noticed an interesting pattern of growth in the total number of rubas on the chessboard as the number of the square increases. Describe the pattern.

c. Write an equation for the relationship between the number of the square, n, and the total number of rubas on the board, t.

d. When the total number of rubas reaches 1,000,000, how many squares will have been covered?

e. If the king had been able to give the peasant the reward she requested, how many rubas would she have received?

Mathematical Reflections

In this investigation, you looked at several situations involving exponential growth. You learned how to recognize patterns of exponential growth in tables, graphs, and equations. These questions will help you summarize what you have learned:

1 Based on your work in this investigation, what do you think are the key properties of exponential growth patterns? How are exponential growth patterns different from the linear patterns you have worked with in earlier units?

2 Consider the exponential equation $y = 2^x$.

    a. How can you calculate the value of y for a given value of x?

    b. Describe the graph of $y = 2^x$.

3 Consider the exponential equation $y = 3^x$.

    a. How is the method of calculating a y value for a given x value for $y = 3^x$ similar to calculating a y value for a given x value for $y = 2^x$? How is it different?

    b. How is a table of values for $y = 3^x$ similar to a table of values for $y = 2^x$? How is it different?

    c. How is the graph of $y = 3^x$ similar to the graph of $y = 2^x$? How is it different?

Think about your answers to these questions, discuss your ideas with other students and your teacher, and then write a summary of your findings in your journal.

Growth Patterns

Now that you have learned to recognize exponential growth, you are ready to take a closer look at the tables, graphs, and equations of exponential relationships. In this investigation, you will explore these questions:

- If the values of a variable grow exponentially, how do they change from one stage to the next?
- How are the starting values and the size of the growth reflected in the table, the graph, and the equation for an exponential relationship?

2.1 Getting Costs in Line

Before presenting plans 2 and 3 to the peasant, the king consulted with his financial advisors. They told the king that either plan would devastate the royal treasury, and they proposed a fourth plan. Under plan 4, the king would put 20 rubas on the first square of a chessboard, 25 on the second, 30 on the third, and so on, increasing the number of rubas by 5 for each square, until all 64 squares were covered.

To help convince the peasant to accept their plan, the advisors prepared the table and graph below comparing the new offer to the original plan. The king presented the plan to the peasant and gave her a day to consider the offer.

	Number of rubas	
Square	Plan 1	Plan 4
1	1	20
2	2	25
3	4	30
4	8	35
5	16	40
6	32	45

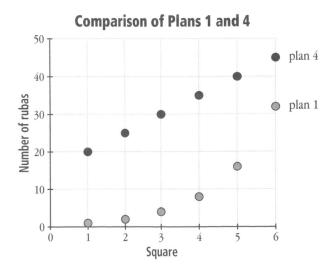

Comparison of Plans 1 and 4

Problem 2.1

A. Make a table showing the number of rubas on squares 7, 8, 9, and 10 for plans 1 and 4.

B. For plan 4, write an equation for the relationship between the number of the square, *n*, and the number of rubas, *r*. How is this equation similar to the equation for plan 1? How is it different?

C. For plans 1 and 4, how many rubas would be on square 20? How many rubas would be on square 30?

D. Write a paragraph explaining why the peasant should or should not accept the king's new offer.

▪ Problem 2.1 Follow-Up

As you compared the reward plans, you probably discovered at least two methods for calculating the number of rubas on a given square: you can use an equation, or you can figure out how the number of rubas changes from one square to the next.

1. For plan 1, there would be 16,384 rubas on square 15. How many rubas would there be on square 16?

2. For plan 4, there would be 90 rubas on square 15. How many rubas would there be on square 16?

3. a. How does the number of rubas change from one square to the next for plan 1?
   b. How does the number of rubas change from one square to the next for plan 4?

4. How are your answers to question 3 represented in the equations for the plans?

2.2 Listening to the Queen

After considering plan 4, the peasant was convinced that the reward under plan 4 was not nearly as large as the original reward she had requested. She went to see the king and queen and politely refused the new offer.

The queen quickly devised yet another plan:

"The king will use a board with 16 squares. He will place 500 rubas on the first square, 1000 on the second, 2000 on the third, 4000 on the fourth, and so on, doubling the number of rubas on each square. As you can see, this plan starts with 500 rubas on the first square and your plan starts with only 1. Surely, you will accept this new offer."

Problem 2.2

A. Make a table showing the number of rubas on squares 5 to 16 for the queen's new plan.

B. Write an equation for the relationship between the number of the square, *n*, and the number of rubas, *r*, for the queen's new plan.

C. Write a paragraph explaining why the peasant should or should not accept the queen's offer.

■ **Problem 2.2 Follow-Up**

1. The king thinks the peasant will be more likely to accept a plan if there are many rubas on the first square. He proposes placing 5 million rubas on the first square of a 16-square board, 6 million on the second square, 7 million on the third, and so on, increasing the number of rubas by 1 million for each square.

   a. Write an equation for the relationship between the number of the square, *n*, and the number of rubas, *r*, for this plan.

   b. Is the relationship between the number of the square and the number of rubas linear or exponential? Explain.

   c. Would you advise the peasant to accept this offer? Why or why not?

2. Make up two reward plans that you think would be hard to choose between. Describe how you designed your plans so that choosing would be difficult. Show your plans to someone and ask which plan he or she would choose.

3. Write an ending to the story of the king and the peasant.

2.3 Growing Mold

Some living organisms grow or reproduce exponentially. Mold, for example, can spread rapidly. The area covered by mold on a loaf of bread left out in warm weather might grow in a pattern like the one shown in the table.

Day	Mold area (cm^2)
0 (start)	1
1	3
2	9
3	27
4	81

Problem 2.3

Look at the pattern in the (day, mold area) data.

   A. Describe how the mold area changes from one day to the next.

   B. Write an equation for the mold area, *A*, after *d* days.

   C. How is your answer to part A reflected in your equation?

Problem 2.3 Follow-Up

Suppose that on day 0, a patch of bread mold has an area of 25 mm^2 (one fourth of a square centimeter) and that the mold grows in the same exponential way it did in Problem 2.3.

1. Copy and complete the table to show the growth of the mold area.

Day	Mold area (mm^2)
0 (start)	25
1	
2	
3	
4	

2. Write an equation for the mold area, A, after d days.

3. Which part of your equation indicates the starting value? Which part indicates the change from one day to the next?

You have looked at several examples of exponential growth patterns. You explored the growth in

- the area of a patch of mold with each day
- the number of rubas with each square
- the number of ballots with each cut

In each case, you found that the value for any stage—day, square, or cut—could be determined by multiplying the value for the previous stage by a fixed number. This fixed number is called the **growth factor.**

4. Give the growth factor for each situation.
   a. making ballots by repeatedly cutting stacks of paper in half
   b. reward plan 1 (Problem 1.2)
   c. reward plan 2 (Problem 1.3)
   d. the growth of bread mold (Problem 2.3)

5. Ilan's biology class did an experiment with bread mold. They wrote the equation $A = 50(3^d)$ to represent the area in mm^2 of the mold after d days.
   a. What was the area of the patch of mold at the start of the experiment?
   b. What was the growth factor?
   c. What was the area of the mold after 5 days?
   d. On which day did the area of the mold reach 10 cm^2?

As you work on these ACE questions, use your calculator whenever you need it.

Applications

1. If you don't brush your teeth regularly, it won't take long for large colonies of bacteria to grow in your mouth. Suppose that a single bacterium lands on one of your teeth and starts reproducing by a factor of 4 every hour.

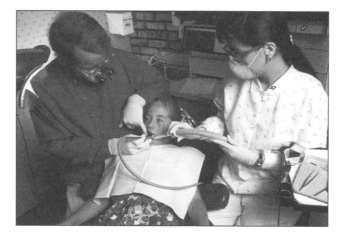

    a. Write an equation that describes the number of bacteria, b, in the new colony after n hours.

    b. How many bacteria will be in the new colony after 7 hours?

    c. How many bacteria will be in the new colony after 8 hours? Explain how you can find this answer by using the answer from part b rather than the equation.

    d. After how many hours will there be at least 1 million bacteria in the colony?

    e. Suppose that 50 bacteria, not just 1 bacterium, land in your mouth. Write an equation that describes the number of bacteria, b, in this colony after n hours.

    f. Under the conditions of part e, there will be 3,276,800 bacteria in this new colony after 8 hours. How many bacteria will there be after 9 hours? After 10 hours? Explain how you can find these answers without using the equation from part e.

2. As a biology project, Nicole is investigating how fast a particular beetle population will grow under controlled conditions. She started her experiment with 5 beetles. The next month she counted 15 beetles.

a. If the beetle population is growing linearly, how many beetles can Nicole expect to find after 2, 3, and 4 months?

b. If the beetle population is growing exponentially, how many beetles can Nicole expect to find after 2, 3, and 4 months?

c. Write an equation for the relationship between the number of beetles and the number of months if the beetle population is growing linearly.

d. Write an equation for the relationship between the number of beetles and the number of months if the beetle population is growing exponentially.

e. If the beetle population is growing linearly, how long will it take the population to reach 200?

f. If the beetle population is growing exponentially, how long will it take the population to reach 200?

3. One of the plans considered by the king's financial advisors involved putting 100 rubas on the first square of a chessboard, 125 on the second square, 150 on the third square, and so on, increasing the number of rubas by 25 for each square until all 64 squares were filled.

a. Write an equation for the numbers of rubas, r, on square n for this plan.

b. How would you expect the graph of this plan to look?

c. What would be the total number of rubas on the first 10 squares? On the first 20 squares?

4. Leaping Leonard just signed a contract with the Peoria Panthers basketball team. The contract guarantees him $20,000 the first year, $40,000 the second year, $80,000 the third year, $160,000 the fourth year, and so on, for 10 years.

    a. Make a table showing Leonard's salary each year of this contract.

    b. What is the total amount of money Leonard will earn in 10 years?

    c. Write an equation relating Leonard's salary, S, and the year, n, of his contract.

Connections

In 5–8, study the pattern in the table. Tell whether the relationship between x and y is linear, exponential, or neither, and explain your answer. If the relationship is linear or exponential, write an equation for the relationship.

5.

x	0	1	2	3	4	5
y	1	4	7	10	13	16

6.

x	0	1	2	3	4
y	1	6	36	216	1296

7.

x	0	1	2	3	4	5	6	7	8
y	1	5	3	7	5	8	6	10	8

8.

x	0	1	2	3	4	5	6	7	8
y	7	14	28	56	112	224	448	896	1792

9. Fido did not have fleas when his owners took him to the kennel. The number of fleas on Fido after he returned from the kennel grew according to the equation $f = 8(3^n)$, where f is the number of fleas and n is the number of weeks since he returned from the kennel.

    a. How many fleas did Fido pick up from the dog kennel?

    b. What is the growth factor for the number of fleas?

    c. If this growth continues, how many fleas will Fido have after 10 weeks?

10. Copy the table below, and complete it according to these rules:
- In column A, find each value by adding 10 to the previous value.
- In column B, find each value by multiplying the previous value by 10.

N	A	B
1	7	7
2		
3		
4		
5		

    a. Is the pattern of change in column A linear, exponential, or neither?

    b. Is the pattern of change in column B linear, exponential, or neither?

    c. Write an equation for the relationship between A and N.

    d. Write an equation for the relationship between B and N.

11. Calculators use *scientific notation* to display very large results. For each expression, find the largest whole-number value of n for which your calculator will display the result in standard notation.

    a. 3^n

    b. π^n

    c. 12^n

    d. 237^n

12. The graph on the next page shows the exponential growth of a garter-snake population for 4 years after the population was introduced to a new area.

    a. What is the population in year 2? In year 3? In year 4?

    b. How does the population change from one year to the next?

    c. Use the pattern in your answers from part a to estimate the population in year 1. Explain how you found your answer.

    d. When is the population likely to be greater than 1500?

    e. Assume the population started with one pregnant female. Write an equation relating time, t, in years, and population, P.

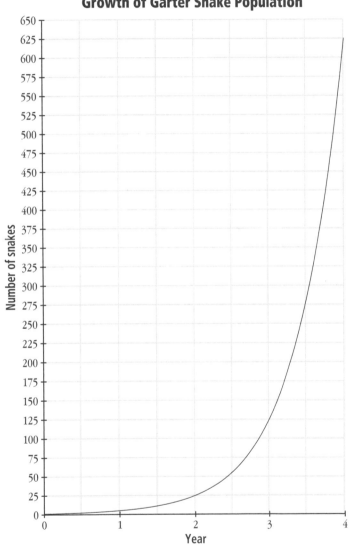

Growth of Garter Snake Population

13. Shahla used a copy machine to enlarge a 2 cm by 3 cm rectangle by a factor of 2 to get a 4 cm by 6 cm rectangle. She then enlarged the 4 cm by 6 cm rectangle by a factor of 2. She continued this process, enlarging each new rectangle by a factor of 2.

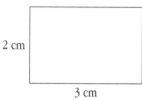

2 cm

3 cm

a. Copy and complete the table to show the area and the perimeter of the rectangle after each enlargement.

Enlargement	Dimensions (cm)	Perimeter (cm)	Area (cm²)
0 (original)	2 by 3		
1	4 by 6		
2			
3			
4			
5			

b. Is the pattern of growth for the perimeter linear, exponential, or neither? Explain your answer.

c. Is the pattern of growth for the area linear, exponential, or neither? Explain your answer.

d. Write an equation for the perimeter, P, after n enlargements.

e. Write an equation for the area, A, after n enlargements.

f. How would your answers to parts a–e change if the copier were set to enlarge by a factor of 3?

14. On the next page are graphs of $y = 2^x$ and $y = 2x + 1$.

a. Which graph is the graph of $y = 2^x$ and which is the graph of $y = 2x + 1$? Explain your answer.

b. The dashed lines show the vertical and horizontal change between points spaced at equal x intervals. For each graph, compare the vertical and horizontal change between each pair of points. What do you notice?

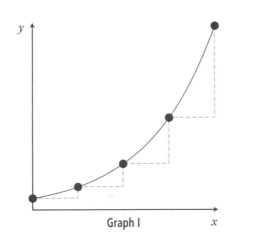

Graph I

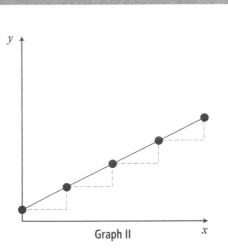

Graph II

Extensions

15. **a.** Copy and complete these tables.

x	2^x
1	
2	
3	
4	
5	

x	4^x
1	
2	
3	
4	
5	

x	8^x
1	
2	
3	
4	
5	

x	2^x
	4096
	16,777,216

x	4^x
	4096
	16,777,216

x	8^x
	4096
	16,777,216

b. What patterns do you see across the tables?

c. Is $2(2^x) = 4^x$? Why or why not?

d. Is $2(4^x) = 8^x$? Why or why not?

16. **a.** Make a table and a graph for the exponential equation $y = 1^x$.

b. How are the patterns in the table and the graph of $y = 1^x$ similar to patterns you have observed for other exponential relationships? How are they different?

Mathematical Reflections

In this investigation, you studied variables with values that grew exponentially. You looked at how the values changed from one stage to the next, and you wrote equations to find the value at any stage. You also compared exponential patterns of change to linear patterns of change. These questions will help you summarize what you have learned:

1 In the equation $y = 5^x$, how does the value of y change each time x increases by 1?

2 How do exponential relationships such as $y = 5^x$ differ from linear relationships such as $y = 5x$ in the way the y value changes as the x value increases?

3 How are graphs and tables of exponential relationships different from those of linear relationships?

4 In the equation $y = a(b^x)$, how does the value of a affect the relationship? For example, how are the table and the graph of $y = 12(5^x)$ different from the table and the graph of $y = 5^x$?

5 Suppose a table for an exponential relationship shows the x value increasing by 1. How can you find the growth factor for the relationship? For example, what is the growth factor for the relationship shown in this table?

x	y
1	343
2	2401
3	16,807
4	117,649

Think about your answers to these questions, discuss your ideas with other students and your teacher, and then write a summary of your findings in your journal.

Growth Factors

In the previous investigations, you studied exponential growth of amoeba, bacterium, snake, and beetle populations. In each case, once you knew the growth factor and the starting population, you could make population predictions. The growth factors in these examples were small whole numbers. In this investigation, you will study examples of exponential growth with fractional growth factors.

3.1 Reproducing Rabbits

In 1859, rabbits were introduced to the island continent of Australia by English settlers who wanted animals they could hunt for sport. The rabbits had no natural predators in Australia, so they reproduced rapidly and became a serious problem, eating grasses intended for sheep and cattle.

Did you know?

A female rabbit can have up to seven litters with five or more rabbits each per year. In 1995, there were over 300 million rabbits in Australia. The damage caused by rabbits costs Australian agriculture $500 million per year. Although there have been many attempts to curb Australia's rabbit population, no method has proven inexpensive or reliable enough to have a significant impact.

If biologists had counted the rabbits in Australia in the years after the rabbits were introduced, they might have collected data like these:

Time (years)	Rabbit population
0	100
1	180
2	325
3	580
4	1050

Problem 3.1

A. The table above shows that the rabbit population grows exponentially. What is the growth factor for this rabbit population? The growth factor from one year to the next is the fraction:

$$\frac{\text{population for year } n}{\text{population for year } n - 1}$$

To find an approximate overall growth factor, compute the growth factors between several pairs of consecutive years and average your results.

B. If this growth pattern had continued, how many rabbits would there have been after 10 years? After 25 years? After 50 years?

C. How many years would it have taken the rabbit population to exceed 1 million?

D. Assume this growth pattern continued. Write an equation you could use to predict the rabbit population, P, for any year, n, after the rabbits were first counted.

Problem 3.1 Follow-Up

After some time, the dangers of the rapid rabbit reproduction became clear to the Australian government, and officials began programs to control the population growth.

1. Suppose that when the rabbit population reached 1 million, the government began control programs that reduced the growth factor to 1.5.
    a. With this growth factor, how many years would it have taken the population to grow from 1 million to 2 million?
    b. How many years would it have taken the population to grow from 1 million to 5 million?
    c. How many years would it have taken the population to grow from 1 million to 10 million?
    d. How many years would it have taken the population to grow from 1 million to 20 million?

2. a. With a growth factor of 1.2, how many years would it have taken the population to double from any starting population?
    b. With a growth factor of 1.5, how many years would it have taken the population to double from any starting population?
    c. With a growth factor of 1.8, how long would it have taken the population to double from any starting population?
    d. What observations can you make about the time it would take the population to double with growth factors of 1.2, 1.5, and 1.8?

3. Suppose that during one time period, the rabbit population could be predicted by the equation $P = 15(1.2^t)$, where P is the population in millions, and t is the number of years.
    a. What does this equation assume about the population growth factor?
    b. What does this equation assume about the initial population?

4. You can think of a growth factor in terms of a percent change. For example, suppose the yearly growth factor for a rabbit population is 1.8.
    • If the initial population is 100 rabbits, there will be 180 rabbits at the end of 1 year.
    • A change from 100 to 180 is an increase of 80 rabbits.
    • Since 80 rabbits is $\frac{80}{100}$, or 80%, of the original population, the rabbit population will increase by 80% each year.
    Find the percent change associated with each growth factor.
    a. 1.5   b. 1.25   c. 1.1

3.2 Investing for the Future

Many people invest their money in land, art, antiques, or other items that will increase in value. Changes in the value of investments are often expressed as percents.

When Sam was in seventh grade, his uncle gave him a coin collection worth $2500. Sam considered selling the collection, but his uncle told him that if he saved it, it would increase in value. Sam saved the collection, and its value increased by 6% each year for several years in a row.

One year after Sam received the coins, their value had increased to $2650.

$$\begin{aligned} \$2500 + (6\% \text{ of } \$2500) &= \$2500 + 0.06(\$2500) \\ &= \$2500 + \$150 \\ &= \$2650 \end{aligned}$$

Two years after Sam received the coins, their value had increased to $2809.

$$\begin{aligned} \$2650 + (6\% \text{ of } \$2650) &= \$2650 + 0.06(2650) \\ &= \$2650 + \$159 \\ &= \$2809 \end{aligned}$$

Sam got very excited when he realized that not only was the value of the coins increasing, but it was increasing by a greater amount each year!

Although the value of the coins increased by the same percent each year, the percent was applied to the current increased value. So, in the second year, the value increased by 6% of $2650, not 6% of the original $2500. This pattern of change is called **compound growth**.

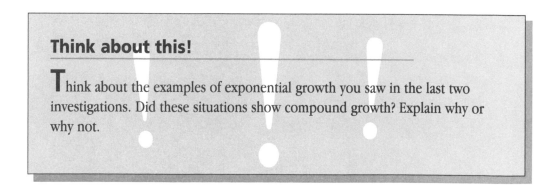

Think about this!

Think about the examples of exponential growth you saw in the last two investigations. Did these situations show compound growth? Explain why or why not.

Problem 3.2

Assume that the value of Sam's coin collection increased by 6% each year for 10 years.

A. Make a table showing the value of the collection each year for the 10 years after Sam's uncle gave it to him.

B. For each year, find the ratio of the value of the coins to the value for the previous year. That is, find

$$\frac{\text{value in year } n}{\text{value in year } n-1}$$

This ratio is the growth factor.

C. Suppose the value of the coins increased by 4% each year instead of 6%.

  1. Make a table showing the value of the collection each year for the 10 years after Sam's uncle gave it to him.

  2. Find the growth factor by examining successive values in the table.

D. What would the growth factor be if the value increased by 5% each year? Explain your answer.

Problem 3.2 Follow-Up

1. How does the reasoning below help explain the growth factor you found for a growth rate of 6%?

next year's value $=$ 100% of this year's value $+$ 6% of this year's value
$\phantom{\text{next year's value}} =$ 106% of this year's value
$\phantom{\text{next year's value}} =$ $1.06 \times$ this year's value

2. Use the reasoning from question 1 to find the growth factor if the value increased by 4% each year. Then, find the growth factor if the value increased by 5% each year. Are the growth factors you found the same as those you found in parts C and D?

3. Sam wrote this formula for calculating the value of the coins t years after he first received them:

$$V = 2500(1.06^t) \quad \text{for } t = 1, 2, 3, \ldots, 10$$

Does Sam's formula give the same results that are in your table for part A?

Making a Difference

Suppose the value of Sam's coin collection increased by 6% each year for 30 years. To find the value of the collection after 30 years, you could make a very long table. A better plan would be to write and solve an equation. In earlier investigations, you used the growth factor and the starting value to help you write equations for exponential growth situations.

Think about this!

Think about how the starting value and the growth factor are used to write the equation in each example below.
- In the reward plan suggested by the peasant in Problem 1.2, 1 ruba would be placed on the first square of a chessboard, and the number of rubas would increase by a factor of 2 with each successive square. The equation for this situation is $r = 1(2^{n-1})$, or simply $r = 2^{n-1}$.
- An experiment began with 25 mm^2 of mold. The area covered by the mold grew by a factor of 3 each day. The equation for this situation is $A = 25(3)^n$.

Problem 3.3

Sam gave some of his coins to his sister to help her pay college expenses. The value of the remaining collection was $1250.

A. Suppose the value of the remaining coins increased by 4% each year. Make a table showing the value of the collection each year for the next 10 years.

B. Sam's friend Maya has a baseball card collection worth $2500. Add a column to your table showing the value of Maya's collection each year for a 10-year period if its value increases by 4% each year.

C. Compare the values of the collections over the 10-year period. How does the initial value of the collection affect the yearly increase in value?

D. How does the initial value of each collection affect the growth factor?

E. Write an equation for the value, V, of Sam's $1250 coin collection after t years.

F. Solve your equation to find the value of Sam's collection after 30 years.

Problem 3.3 Follow-Up

1. Sam made the following calculation to predict the value of his aunt's stamp collection several years from now:

$$\text{value} = \$2400 \times 1.05 \times 1.05 \times 1.05 \times 1.05$$

    a. What initial value, rate of increase in value, and number of years is Sam assuming?

    b. The result of Sam's calculation is $2917.22. If the value continued to increase at this rate, how much would the collection be worth in one more year?

2. Find the growth factor associated with each percent increase.

    a. 30%   **b.** 15%   **c.** 5%   **d.** 75%

As you work on these ACE questions, use your calculator whenever you need it.

Applications

1. In parts of the United States, wolves are being reintroduced to wilderness areas where they have become extinct. Suppose 20 wolves are released in northern Michigan, and the yearly growth factor for this population is expected to be 1.2.

    a. Make a table showing the projected number of wolves at the end of each of the first 6 years.

    b. Write an equation that models the growth pattern of the wolf population.

    c. How long will it take for the new wolf population to exceed 100?

2. Fruit flies *(Drosophila melanogaster)* are often used in genetic experiments because they reproduce at a phenomenal rate. In 12 days, a pair of *Drosophila* can mature and produce a new generation of fruit flies. The table below shows the number of fruit flies in three generations of a laboratory colony.

Generation	0	1	2	3
Number of fruit flies	2	120	7200	432,000

    a. What is the growth factor for this fruit-fly population? Explain how you found your answer.

    b. If this pattern continues, how many fruit flies will there be in the fifth generation?

c. Write an equation for the population, P, of this fruit-fly colony as a function of the generation, g.

d. If the pattern in the table continues, after how many generations will the population exceed 1 million?

3. Currently, 1000 students attend Greenville Day School. The school can accommodate 1300 students. The directors of the school estimate that the student population will grow by 5% per year for the next several years.

a. In how many years will the population outgrow the present building?

b. Suppose the school limits its growth to 50 students per year. How many years will it take for the population to outgrow the present building?

4. Suppose that for several years the number of radios sold in the United States increased by 3% each year.

a. If 1 million radios were sold in the first year of this time period, about how many radios were sold in each of the next 6 years?

b. If 100,000 radios were sold in the first year, about how many radios were sold in each of the next 6 years?

5. Suppose a movie ticket costs about $7, and inflation causes ticket prices to increase by 4% a year.

a. At this rate, how much will a ticket cost 5 years from now?

b. At this rate, how much will a ticket cost 10 years from now?

c. At this rate, how much will a ticket cost 30 years from now?

6. In Russia, shortly after the breakup of the Soviet Union, the growth factor for inflation was 1.5. What percent increase is associated with this growth factor? We call this percent increase the *inflation rate*.

7. If the price of a product increases by 25% per year, what is the growth factor from year to year?

Connections

8. Government workers often get cost-of-living pay raises. Suppose a government worker has an annual salary of $20,000.

a. What would be the dollar value of a 3% raise for this worker? Of a 4% raise? Of a 6% raise?

b. What would the worker's new annual salary be for each raise in part a?

c. You can find the new salary after a 3% raise in two ways:

$20,000 + (3% of $20,000)$ or 103% of $20,000$

Why do these two methods give the same result?

9. After graduating from high school, Kwan accepted a job with a package delivery service, earning $5.15 per hour.

a. How much will Kwan earn in a year if she works 40 hours per week for 50 weeks and gets 2 weeks of paid vacation time?

b. Suppose Kwan works for the company for 10 years, receiving a 3% raise each year. Make a table showing how her annual income grows over this time period.

c. When Kwan was hired, her manager told her that instead of a 3% annual raise, she could choose to receive a $350 raise each year. How do the two raise plans compare over a 10-year period? Which plan do you think is better? Explain your answer.

10. You can evaluate exponential expressions such as 1.25^{10} and 1.5^7 in several ways.

    a. Determine which expressions below are equivalent to 1.25^{10}. Explain why each expression is or is not equivalent.

        i. $1.25^5 \times 1.25^5$ **ii.** $1.25^3 \times 1.25^7$

        iii. 1.25×10 **iv.** $1.25 + 10$

    b. Determine which expressions below are equivalent to 1.5^7. Explain why each expression is or is not equivalent.

        i. $1.5^5 \times 1.5^2$ **ii.** $1.5^3 \times 1.5^4$

        iii. 1.5×7 **iv.** $1.5 + 7$

11. Katrina used a copy machine to enlarge this drawing of a flag to 110% of this size.

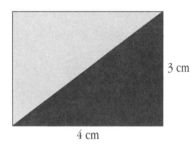

3 cm

4 cm

    a. What are the length of the diagonal and the area of the shaded region of the original drawing?

    b. What are the length of the diagonal and the area of the shaded region of the enlarged drawing?

    c. Katrina enlarged the enlargement to 110% of its size. She continued this process, enlarging each new drawing to 110% of its size. After five enlargements, what were the length of the diagonal and the area of the shaded region?

    d. Is each enlargement similar to the original figure? Explain. (Hint: Compare the ratio of the length to the width for each enlargement to the ratio of the length to the width for the original.)

In 12–14, tell whether the pattern represents exponential growth. Explain your answer.

12.   1   1.1   1.21   1.331   1.4641   1.61051   1.771561

13.   0   3   6   9   12   15   18

14.   2   8   18   32   50   72   98

Extensions

15. In 1990, the population of the United States was about 250 million and was growing exponentially at a rate of about 0.7% per year. (Remember, 0.7% = 0.007.)

    a. At this growth rate, what will the population of the United States be in the year 2000?

    b. At this rate, how long will it take the population to double?

    c. Do you think the predictions in parts a and b are accurate? Explain.

16. The table below gives the world population from 1955 to 1990 in 5-year intervals.

Year	1955	1960	1965	1970	1975	1980	1985	1990
Population (billions)	2.70	2.98	3.29	3.63	4.01	4.43	4.84	5.29

    a. One model of world population growth assumes that the population grows exponentially. Based on the data in this table, what would be a reasonable growth factor for this model?

    b. Use your growth factor to write an equation for the growth of the population at 5-year intervals beginning in 1955.

    c. Use your equation to predict the 5-year interval in which the population will be double the 1955 population.

    d. Use your equation to predict when the population will be double the 1990 population.

17. If your calculator did not have an exponent key ($\boxed{\wedge}$ or $\boxed{y^x}$), you could evaluate 1.5^{12} by entering $1.5 \times 1.5 \times 1.5 \times 1.5 \times 1.5 \times 1.5 \times 1.5 \times 1.5 \times 1.5 \times 1.5 \times 1.5 \times 1.5$.

   a. How could you evaluate 1.5^{12} with fewer keystrokes?

   b. What is the least number of times you could press $\boxed{\times}$ to evaluate 1.5^{12}?

18. The following graph shows the growth in the number of cellular-phone subscribers from 1986 to 1994.

   a. What do the bars in the graph represent?

   b. What does the curve represent?

   c. Describe the pattern of change in the total number of subscribers. Is the pattern exponential? Explain.

Worldwide Cellular Phone Usage

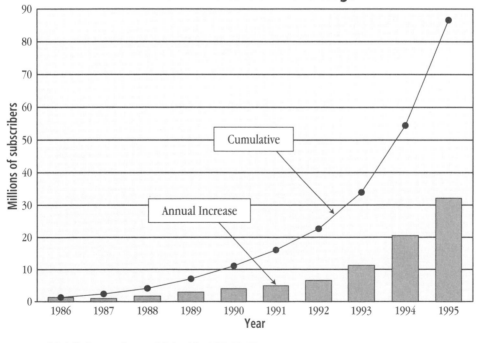

Source: *World Cellular Markets* published by MTA-EMCI

Mathematical Reflections

In this investigation, you explored exponential growth situations in which the growth factor was not a whole number. These questions will help you summarize what you have learned:

1 Suppose you had data about the growth of a fish population in a lake over several years.

    a. How would you decide whether the population was growing exponentially?

    b. If the population growth appeared to be exponential, how would you use the data to write an equation for the growth?

2 How is a growth rate of 20% related to an exponential growth factor of 1.2?

3 Suppose rents in a particular area are increasing by 20% per year.

    a. Predict what an apartment that now rents for $1500 per month will rent for 1 year from now. Explain your work.

    b. Predict what an apartment that now rents for $1500 per month will rent for each year for the next 5 years. Explain your work.

    c. Write an equation that you could use to predict the rent for the $1500 apartment t years from now.

Think about your answers to these questions, discuss your ideas with other students and your teacher, and then write a summary of your findings in your journal.

Exponential Decay

The exponential patterns you have studied so far in this unit have all involved variables with increasing values. In this investigation, you will explore variables with values that decrease, or *decay*, exponentially as time passes.

4.1 Making Smaller Ballots

In Problem 1.1, you read about the ballots that Alejandro was making for an election. Recall that Alejandro cut a sheet of paper in half, stacked the two pieces and cut them in half, and then stacked the resulting four pieces and cut them in half.

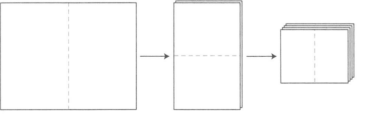

In Problem 1.1, you investigated the pattern in the number of ballots created by each cut. In this problem, you will look at the pattern in the areas of the ballots.

Problem 4.1

Cut a sheet of paper as Alejandro did, and look for a pattern in the area of the ballots after each cut. Use what you discover to help you complete this problem.

A. The sheet of paper Alejandro started with had an area of 64 in². Copy and complete the table below to show the area of a ballot after each of the first 10 cuts.

Cuts	Area (in²)
0	64
1	32
2	16
3	
4	
5	
6	
7	
8	
9	
10	

B. How does the area of a ballot change with each cut?

C. How is the pattern of change in the area different from the exponential growth patterns you have seen in this unit? How is it similar?

■ Problem 4.1 Follow-Up

You may have described the pattern of change in the area of a ballot by saying it is "cut in half" or "divided in two" with each cut. This means that with each cut the area is multiplied by $\frac{1}{2}$, or divided by 2.

The area of the original sheet of paper was 64 in². The first cut multiplies this area by $\frac{1}{2}$, or 0.5:

$$\text{area after 1 cut} = 64 \times 0.5$$

The second cut multiplies the new area by 0.5:

$$\text{area after 2 cuts} = 64 \times 0.5 \times 0.5 = 64(0.5^2)$$

This pattern of multiplying by 0.5 continues with each cut:

$$\text{area after 3 cuts} = 64 \times 0.5 \times 0.5 \times 0.5 = 64(0.5^3)$$
$$\text{area after 4 cuts} = 64 \times 0.5 \times 0.5 \times 0.5 \times 0.5 = 64(0.5^4)$$

$$\cdot$$
$$\cdot$$
$$\cdot$$

The area, A, of a ballot after n cuts can be represented by the equation $A = 64(0.5^n)$. Notice that this is an exponential equation similar to the equations you have worked with in previous investigations.

We say that exponential patterns like this, in which the quantity *decreases* with each stage, show **exponential decay**. We call the factor we multiply by at each stage the **decay factor.** In the example above, the decay factor is 0.5. While a growth factor is always greater than 1, a decay factor is always less than 1.

Suppose you start with a sheet of paper with an area of 27 in^2. Instead of cutting the stack of paper in half at each stage, you cut it into thirds:

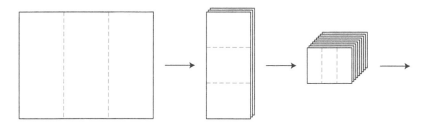

1. Copy and complete the table below to show the area of a ballot at each stage.

Stage	Area (cm^2)
0	27
1	9
2	
3	
4	
5	
6	

2. How does the area of a ballot change at each stage?

3. Write an equation for the area, A, of a ballot at any stage, n.

4. Make a graph of the (stage, area) data from your table.

After a dog or cat is given a preventive flea medicine, the medicine begins to break down in the animal's bloodstream. With each passing hour, there is less active medicine in the blood. The table and the graph below show the amount of active medicine in a dog's bloodstream each hour for 6 hours after a 20-milligram dose.

Time since dose (hours)	Active medicine in blood (milligrams)
0	20
1	10
2	5
3	2.5
4	1.25
5	0.625
6	0.3125

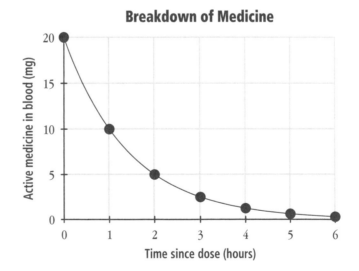

Breakdown of Medicine

Problem 4.2

Study the pattern of change in the graph and the table.

A. How does the amount of active medicine in the dog's blood change from one hour to the next?

B. Write an equation to model the relationship between the number of hours since the dose was administered, h, and the milligrams of active medicine, m.

C. Based on your knowledge of exponential relationships, what pattern would you expect to see in the data if 40 milligrams of the medicine were given to the dog?

Problem 4.2 Follow-Up

1. Suppose that, after an initial dose of 60 milligrams, a flea medicine breaks down at a rate of 20% per hour in an animal's bloodstream. This means that as each hour passes, 20% of the active medicine is used. Copy and complete the table to show the amount of active medicine in an animal's blood at the end of each hour for 6 hours.

Time since dose (hours)	Active medicine in blood (milligrams)
0	60
1	
2	
3	
4	
5	
6	

2. For the medicine described in question 1, Janelle wrote the equation $m = 60(0.8^h)$ to model the relationship between the amount of medicine in the blood and the number of hours since it was administered. Compare the quantities of active medicine in your table to the quantities given by Janelle's equation for several time values. Explain any similarities or differences you find.

3. Janelle's friend Habib was confused by the terms *rate of decay* and *decay factor*. He said that since the rate of decay in question 1 is 20%, the decay factor should be 0.2 and the equation should be $m = 60(0.2^h)$. How would you explain to Habib why a rate of decay of 20% is equivalent to a decay factor of 0.8?

4.3 Exploring Exponential Equations

In this unit, you have studied situations that show patterns of exponential growth or exponential decay. All of these situations are modeled by equations of the form $y = a(b^x)$, where a is the starting value and b is the growth or decay factor. You can use your graphing calculator to explore how the values of a and b affect the graph of $y = a(b^x)$.

Problem 4.3

In this problem, you will let $a = 1$ and explore how the value of b affects the graph of $y = b^x$.

A. Use your calculator to investigate the equation $y = b^x$ for $b = 1.25, 1.5, 1.75,$ and 2. That is, investigate these equations:

$$y = 1.25^x \qquad y = 1.5^x \qquad y = 1.75^x \qquad y = 2^x$$

Graph all four equations in the same window. Use window settings that show x values from 0 to 5 and y values from 0 to 20. Record your observations.

B. Use your calculator to investigate the equation $y = b^x$ for $b = 0.25, 0.5,$ and 0.75. That is, investigate these equations:

$$y = 0.25^x \qquad y = 0.5^x \qquad y = 0.75^x$$

Use window settings that show $0 \le x \le 5$ and $0 \le y \le 1$. Record your observations.

C. Based on your explorations in parts A and B, describe how you could predict the general shape of the graph of $y = b^x$ for a specific value of b.

Problem 4.3 Follow-Up

In parts A and B, you explored how the value of b affects the graph of $y = b^x$. Now, you will look at how the value of a affects the graph of $y = a(b^x)$. You will need to adjust the window settings as you work.

1. Use your calculator to explore the equation $y = a(2^x)$ for $a = 2, 3,$ and 4. That is, investigate these equations:

$$y = 2(2^x) \qquad y = 3(2^x) \qquad y = 4(2^x)$$

2. Use your calculator to explore the equation $y = a(1.5^x)$ for $a = 2, 3,$ and 4. That is, investigate these equations:

$$y = 2(1.5^x) \qquad y = 3(1.5^x) \qquad y = 4(1.5^x)$$

Record your observations.

3. Use your calculator to explore the equation $y = a(0.5^x)$ for $a = 2, 3,$ and 4. That is, investigate these equations:

$$y = 2(0.5^x) \qquad y = 3(0.5^x) \qquad y = 4(0.5^x)$$

Record your observations.

4. Describe how the value of a affects the graph of an equation of the form $y = a(b^x)$.

 ## Cooling Water

Have you ever sipped from a cup of hot cocoa or tea and found that it was too hot to drink? What pattern of change would you expect to find in the temperature of a hot drink as time passes? What shape would you expect for a graph of (time, drink temperature) data? This experiment will help you explore these questions.

Equipment:
* very hot water, a thermometer, a cup or mug for hot drinks, and a watch or clock

Directions:
* Record the air temperature.
* Fill the cup with hot water.
* In a table, record the water temperature and the room temperature in 5-minute intervals throughout your class period.

Time (minutes)	Water temperature	Room temperature
0		
5		
10		

Problem 4.4

A. Make a graph of your (time, water temperature) data.

B. Describe the pattern of change in the (time, water temperature) data. When did the water temperature change most rapidly? When did it change most slowly?

C. Add a column to your table. In this column, record the difference between the water temperature and the room temperature for each time value.

D. Make a graph of the (time, temperature difference) data.

E. Compare the shapes of the graphs.

F. Describe the pattern of change in the (time, temperature difference) data. When did the temperature difference change most rapidly? When did it change most slowly?

G. Assume that the relationship between temperature difference and time in this experiment is exponential. Estimate the decay factor for this relationship. Explain how you made your estimate.

H. Find an equation for the (time, temperature difference) data. Your equation should allow you to predict the temperature difference at the end of any 5-minute interval.

Problem 4.4 Follow-Up

1. What do you think the graph of the (time, temperature difference) data would look like if you had continued the experiment for several more hours?

2. What factors might affect the rate at which a cup of hot liquid cools?

3. What factors might introduce errors in the data you collect?

As you work on these ACE questions, use your calculator whenever you need it.

Applications

1. Rosemary often shares her snacks with her friends. One day she had a 24-inch string of licorice. As each friend asked her for a piece, Rosemary gave him or her half of what she had left.

   a. Make a table showing the amount of licorice Rosemary had left each time she gave a piece away.

   b. Make a graph of the data from part a.

   c. Suppose that, instead of half the licorice, Rosemary gave each friend 4 inches of licorice. Make a table and a graph for this situation.

   d. Compare the tables and the graphs for the two situations. Explain the similarities and the differences.

2. Penicillin decays exponentially in the human body. If you receive a 300-milligram dose of penicillin to combat strep throat, about 180 milligrams will still be active in your blood after one day.

   a. Assume the amount of active penicillin in your blood decreases exponentially. Make a table showing the amount of penicillin remaining active in your blood each day for 7 days after a 300-milligram dose.

   b. Write an equation for the relationship between the number of days, d, since you took the penicillin and the amount of the medicine, m, remaining active in your body.

   c. How would the equation change if you had taken a 400-milligram dose?

3. In a class experiment, hot coffee was poured into a cup and allowed to cool. The difference between coffee temperature and room temperature was recorded every minute for 10 minutes.

Time (minutes)	0	1	2	3	4	5	6	7	8	9	10
Temperature difference (°C)	80	72	65	58	52	47	43	38	34	31	28

a. Plot the (time, temperature difference) data. Explain what the patterns in the table and the graph tell you about the rate at which the coffee cooled.

b. Approximate the decay factor for this relationship.

c. Write an equation for the relationship between time and temperature difference.

d. About how long would it have taken the coffee to cool to room temperature? Explain how you found your answer.

Connections

4. a. The pizza in the ad for Mr. Costa's restaurant has a diameter of 5 inches. What are the circumference and the area of the pizza in the ad?

b. On most copy machines, reduction settings are given as percents. A setting of 90% reduces a drawing to 90% of its original size. Mr. Costa reduces his ad to 90% of its original size. He then reduces the reduced ad to 90% of its size. He continues this process, performing a total of five reductions. Copy and complete the table to show the diameter, circumference, and area of the pizza after each reduction.

Reduction	Diameter (in)	Circumference (in)	Area (in^2)
0			
1			
2			
3			
4			
5			

c. Write equations for the diameter, the circumference, and the area of the pizza after n reductions.

d. How would your equations change if Mr. Costa had used a reduction setting of 75%?

e. Mr. Costa claims that when he uses the 90% reduction setting, he is actually reducing the size of the drawing by 10%. Is Mr. Costa correct? Explain.

5. Consider these three equations:

$$y = 0.75^x \qquad y = 0.25^x \qquad y = {}^-0.5x + 1$$

a. Sketch the graphs of all three equations on one set of axes.

b. What points, if any, do the three graphs have in common?

c. In which graph does the y value decrease at the greatest rate as the x value increases?

d. How can you use your graphs to determine which of the equations is *not* an example of exponential decay?

e. How can you use the equations to determine which one is *not* an example of exponential decay?

6. A cricket is on the 0 point of a number line, hopping toward 1. She covers half the distance from her current location to 1 with each hop. So, she will be at $\frac{1}{2}$ after one hop, $\frac{3}{4}$ after two hops, and so on.

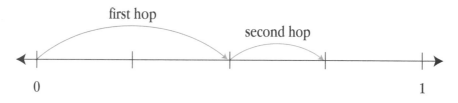

a. Make a table showing the cricket's location for the first 10 hops.

b. Where will the cricket be after n hops?

c. Will the cricket ever get to 1? Explain.

Extensions

7. Negative numbers can be used as exponents. This question will help you to understand negative exponents.

a. Consider the equation $y = 2^x$. Use your calculator to find the value of y for x values $^-1$, $^-2$, and $^-3$.

b. Consider the equation $y = (\frac{1}{2})^x$. Compute the value of y for x values 1, 2, and 3.

c. What observation can you make from your computations in parts a and b?

8. Freshly-cut lumber, known as *green lumber,* contains water. If green lumber is used to build a house, it may crack, shrink, and warp as it dries. To avoid these problems, green lumber is typically dried in a kiln that circulates dry air to remove moisture from the wood. Suppose that in one week a kiln removes $\frac{1}{3}$ of the moisture from a stack of lumber.

    a. What fraction of the moisture *remains* in the lumber after 5 weeks?

    b. What fraction of the moisture has been *removed* from the lumber after 5 weeks?

    c. Write an equation for the fraction of moisture remaining in the lumber after w weeks.

    d. Write an equation for the fraction of moisture that has been removed from the lumber after w weeks.

    e. Graph your equations from parts c and d on the same set of axes. Describe how the graphs are related.

    f. A different kiln removes $\frac{1}{4}$ of the moisture from a stack of lumber each week. Write equations for the fraction of moisture remaining and the fraction of moisture removed after w weeks.

    g. Graph your two equations from part f on the same set of axes. Describe how the graphs are related. How do they compare to the graphs from part e?

    h. Suppose a batch of green lumber is 40% water by weight and a builder wants its moisture content to be 10%. For each of the two kilns described above, how long should the lumber be dried before it is used to build the house?

9. Study this pattern:

row 1: $\frac{1}{2} =$

row 2: $\frac{1}{2} + (\frac{1}{2})^2 =$

row 3: $\frac{1}{2} + (\frac{1}{2})^2 + (\frac{1}{2})^3 =$

row 4: $\frac{1}{2} + (\frac{1}{2})^2 + (\frac{1}{2})^3 + (\frac{1}{2})^4 =$

a. Find the sum for each row.

b. Suppose the pattern continued. Write the expression that would be in row 5, and find its sum.

c. What would be the sum of the expression in row 10? In row 20?

d. Describe the pattern of sums in words and with an equation.

e. For which row does the sum first exceed 0.9?

f. As the row number increases, the sum gets closer and closer to what number?

g. Celeste claims that the pattern is related to the pattern of the areas of the ballots cut in Problem 4.1. She drew this picture to explain her thinking.

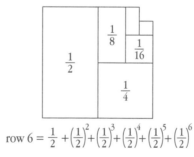

$$\text{row } 6 = \frac{1}{2} + \left(\frac{1}{2}\right)^2 + \left(\frac{1}{2}\right)^3 + \left(\frac{1}{2}\right)^4 + \left(\frac{1}{2}\right)^5 + \left(\frac{1}{2}\right)^6$$

What relationship do you think Celeste has observed?

10. Study this pattern:

row 1: $\frac{1}{3} =$

row 2: $\frac{1}{3} + (\frac{1}{3})^2 =$

row 3: $\frac{1}{3} + (\frac{1}{3})^2 + (\frac{1}{3})^3 =$

row 4: $\frac{1}{3} + (\frac{1}{3})^2 + (\frac{1}{3})^3 + (\frac{1}{3})^4 =$

a. Find the sum for each row.

b. Suppose the pattern continued. Write the expression that would be in row 5, and find its sum.

c. What would be the sum of the expression in row 10? In row 20?

d. Describe the pattern of sums in words and with an equation.

e. For which row does the sum first exceed 0.9?

f. As the row number increases, the sum gets closer and closer to what number?

Mathematical Reflections

In this investigation, you explored situations that showed patterns of exponential decay. These questions will help you summarize what you have learned:

1 How can you recognize an exponential decay pattern from a table of data? From a graph? From an equation?

2 How is a table for an exponential decay situation different from a table for an exponential growth situation? How is the graph different? How is the equation different?

3 How are patterns in tables, graphs, and equations for exponential decay situations similar to and different from tables, graphs, and equations for decreasing linear relationships?

Think about your answers to these questions, discuss your ideas with other students and your teacher, and then write a summary of your findings in your journal.

Half-Life

Most of the objects and substances around you are composed of atoms that are stable. However, the atoms that make up *radioactive* substances are unstable—they tend to break down in a process known as *radioactive decay*. As these substances decay, they emit radiation. At high levels, radiation can be dangerous to humans and other living creatures.

The rate of decay varies from substance to substance. Scientists use the term *half-life* to describe the time it takes for half of the atoms in a radioactive sample to decay. For example, the half-life of carbon-11 is 20 minutes. This means that 2000 carbon-11 atoms will be reduced to 1000 carbon-11 atoms in 20 minutes and to 500 carbon-11 atoms in 40 minutes.

Half-lives vary from a fraction of a second to billions of years. For example, the half-life of polonium-214 is 0.00016 seconds, and the half-life of rubidium-87 is 49 billion years.

In this experiment, you will model the decay of a radioactive substance known as iodine-124. About $\frac{1}{6}$ of the atoms in a sample of iodine-124 decay each day. This experiment will help you determine the half-life of this substance.

Follow these steps to conduct your experiment:

- Use 100 cubes to represent 100 iodine-124 atoms. Mark one face of each cube.
- Place all 100 cubes in a container, shake the container, and pour the cubes onto the table.
- The cubes for which the mark is facing up represent atoms that have decayed on the first day. Remove these cubes, and record the number of cubes that remain. Place the remaining cubes in the container.

- Repeat this process to find the number of atoms that remain after the second day.
- Repeat this process until one cube or no cubes remain.

When you complete your experiment, answer these questions:

1 a. In your experiment, how many days did it take to reduce the 100 iodine-124 atoms to 50 atoms? In other words, how many times did you have to roll the cubes until about 50 cubes remained?

b. How many days did it take to reduce 50 iodine-124 atoms to 25 atoms?

c. Based on your answers to parts a and b, what do you think the half life of iodine-124 is?

2 a. In a sample of real iodine-124, $\frac{1}{6}$ of the atoms decay after 1 day. What fraction of the atoms remain after 1 day?

b. Suppose a sample contains 100 iodine-124 atoms. Use your answer from part a to write an equation for the number of atoms, n, remaining in the sample after d days.

c. Use your equation to find the half-life of iodine-124.

d. How does the half-life you found based on your equation compare to the half-life you found from your experiment?

3 a. Make up a problem about a radioactive substance with a different rate of decay that can be modeled by an experiment involving cubes or other common objects. Describe the situation and your experiment.

b. Conduct your experiment, and record your results.

c. Use the results of your experiment to predict the half-life of your substance.

d. Use what you know about the rate of decay to write an equation that models the decay of your substance.

e. Use your equation to find the half-life of your substance.

Write a report summarizing your findings about decay rates and half-lives. Your report should include tables and graphs justifying your answers to the questions above.

Looking Back and Looking Ahead

Unit Reflections

Working on the problems of this unit expanded your skill in recognizing and using *exponential* relationships among variables. You used equations in the form $y = a(b^x)$ to describe exponential *growth* of various populations and investments and *decay* of medicines and radioactive materials. You used those equations to produce tables and graphs of the relations. Then the tables and graphs were used to make predictions and solve equations.

Using Your Algebraic Reasoning—To test your understanding and skill in finding and applying exponential models, consider the following questions that arose when the Student Council at Spartan Middle School planned some entertainment for a fund-raising event. One popular idea was to sponsor a quiz show called "Who Wants To Be Rich?" The general idea was that as questions increased in difficulty, the prize package increased as well.

1 *One proposal was to have the first question worth $5 and to have the total prize increase by $10 for each additional question answered correctly.*

   a. What equation gives the prize, P, for correctly answering questions 1 to n?

   b. How many questions will a contestant need to answer correctly in order to win $50? $75? $100?

   c. Sketch a graph of the proposal data for $0 \le n \le 10$.

2 *A second proposal was to have the first question worth $5 and to have the contestant's total winnings double for each additional question answered correctly.*

   a. What equation gives the prize, P, for correctly answering questions 1 to n?

   b. How many questions will a contestant need to answer correctly in order to win $50? $75? $100?

   c. Sketch a graph of this proposal data for $0 \le n \le 10$.

3 *Contestants for "Who Wants to Be Rich?" would be chosen by a drawing. Students and guests at the fund-raiser would buy tickets like the one shown below. The purchaser would keep one half of the ticket and add the other half to the entries for the drawing.*

a. To make the tickets, the event's planners took a large piece of paper and folded it in half many times to make a grid of small rectangles. How many such rectangles were there after *n* folds?

b. If the original piece of paper for tickets was a 60-cm square, what is the area for each ticket rectangle after *n* folds?

Explaining Your Reasoning—To answer the questions about the game plans, you had to use algebraic knowledge about number patterns, graphs, and equations or formulas. You had to recognize linear and exponential patterns and find matching equations and graphs.

1. How do you decide when a data pattern can be modeled well by an exponential equation in the form $y = a(b^x)$? How will the values of *a* and *b* relate to the data pattern?

2. What are the possible shapes of graphs for exponential relations and how can they be predicted from values of *a* and *b* in the corresponding equations?

3. How are the data patterns, graphs, and symbolic equations in exponential relations you studied similar to and different from those modeled by linear equations?

The algebra ideas and techniques you've used in this unit will be applied and extended in future units of *Connected Mathematics* and in problems of science and business. You'll study several other important families of algebraic models and strategies for finding and using those models to solve problems.

Glossary

base The number that is raised to a power in an exponential expression. In the expression 3^5, read "3 to the fifth power," 3 is the base and 5 is the exponent.

compound growth Another term for exponential growth, usually used when talking about the monetary value of an investment. The change in the balance of a savings account shows compound growth because the bank pays interest not only on the original investment, but on the interest earned.

decay factor The constant factor that each value in an exponential decay pattern is multiplied by to get the next value. The decay factor is the base in an exponential decay equation. For example, in the equation $A = 64(0.5^n)$, where A is the area of a ballot and n is the number of cuts, the decay factor is 0.5. It indicates that the area of a ballot after any number of cuts is 0.5 times the area after the previous number of cuts. In a table of (x, y) values for an exponential decay relationship (with the x value increasing by 1), the decay factor is the ratio of any y value to the previous y value.

exponent A number that indicates how many times another number (the base) is to be used as a factor. Exponents are written as raised numbers to the right of the base. In the expression 3^5, read "3 to the fifth power," 5 is the exponent and 3 is the base. So, 3^5 means $3 \times 3 \times 3 \times 3 \times 3$. In the formula for the area of a square, $A = s^2$, the 2 is an exponent. This formula can also be written as $A = s \times s$.

exponential decay A pattern of decrease in which each value is found by multiplying the previous value by a constant factor greater than 0 and less than 1. For example, the pattern 27, 9, 3, 1, $\frac{1}{3}$, $\frac{1}{9}$, . . . shows exponential decay in which each value is $\frac{1}{3}$ times the previous value.

exponential form A quantity expressed as a number raised to a power. In exponential form, 32 can be written as 2^5.

exponential growth A pattern of increase in which each value is found by multiplying the previous value by a constant factor greater than 1. For example, the pattern 1, 2, 4, 8, 16, 32, . . . shows exponential growth in which each value is 2 times the previous value.

growth factor The constant factor that each value in an exponential growth pattern is multiplied by to get the next value. The growth factor is the base in an exponential growth equation. For example, in the equation $A = 25(3^d)$, where A is the area of a patch of mold and d is the number of days, the growth factor is 3. It indicates that the area of the mold for any day is 3 times the area for the previous day. In a table of (x, y) values for an exponential growth relationship (with x the value increasing by 1), the growth factor is the ratio of any y value to the previous y value.

standard form The most common way to express a quantity. For example, 27 is the standard form of 3^3.

Index